ALABAMA

Karen Durrie

www.av2books.com

Go to **www.av2books.com**, and enter this book's unique code.

BOOK CODE

M 3 1 8 2 2 7

AV² by Weigl brings you media enhanced books that support active learning.

AV² provides enriched content that supplements and complements this book. Weigl's AV² books strive to create inspired learning and engage young minds in a total learning experience.

Your AV² Media Enhanced books come alive with...

Audio
Listen to sections of the book read aloud.

Video
Watch informative video clips.

Embedded Weblinks
Gain additional information for research.

Try This!
Complete activities and hands-on experiments.

Key Words
Study vocabulary, and complete a matching word activity.

Quizzes
Test your knowledge.

Slide Show
View images and captions, and prepare a presentation.

... and much, much more!

Published by AV² by Weigl
350 5th Avenue, 59th Floor
New York, NY 10118
Website: www.av2books.com   www.weigl.com

Library of Congress Cataloging-in-Publication Data
Durrie, Karen.
 Alabama / Karen Durrie.
    p. cm. -- (Explore the U.S.A.)
Includes bibliographical references and index.
ISBN 978-1-61913-321-1 (hard cover : alk. paper)
1. Alabama--Juvenile literature. I. Title.
F326.3.D87 2012
976.1--dc23
                              2012015067

Printed in the United States of America in North Mankato, Minnesota
1 2 3 4 5 6 7 8 9 16 15 14 13 12

052012
WEP040512

Project Coordinator: Karen Durrie
Art Director: Terry Paulhus

Weigl acknowledges Getty Images as the primary image supplier for this title.

ALABAMA

Contents

2   AV² Book Code
4   Nickname
6   Location
8   History
10 Flower and Seal
12 Flag
14 Bird
16 Capital
18 Goods
20 Fun Things to Do
22 Facts
24 Key Words

3

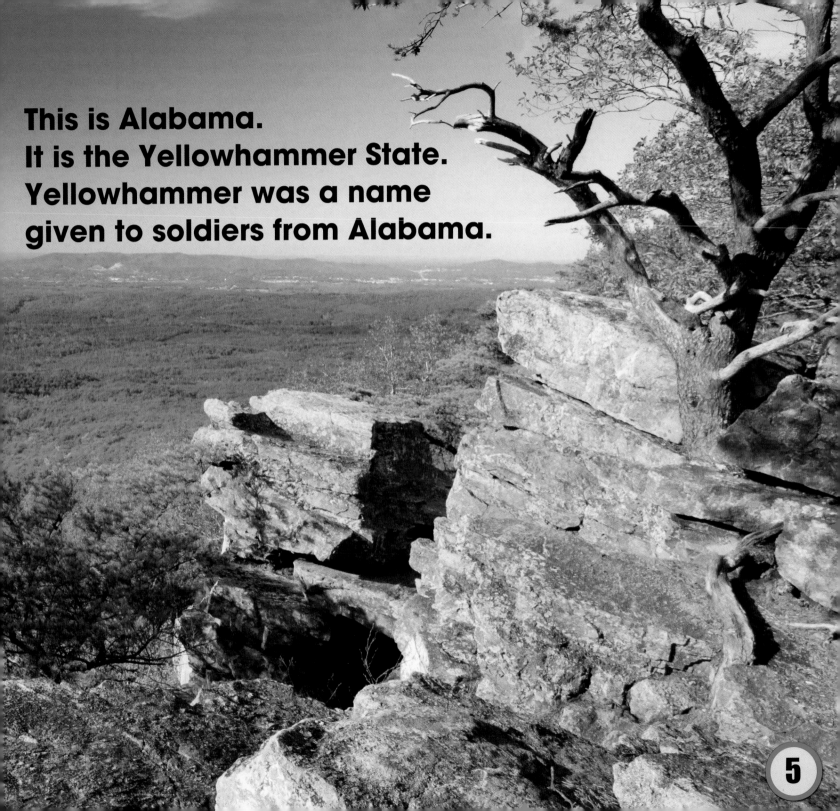

This is Alabama.
It is the Yellowhammer State.
Yellowhammer was a name
given to soldiers from Alabama.

This is the shape of Alabama. It is in the south part of the United States. Four states border Alabama.

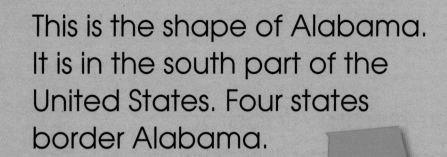

Where is Alabama?

Canada

N
W   E
S

Pacific Ocean

United States

Atlantic Ocean

Mexico   Gulf of Mexico

Alabama is next to the Gulf of Mexico.

Workers from Alabama built the first rocket that took people to the Moon.

The rocket went from Earth to space in less than three minutes.

The camellia is the Alabama state flower. Explorers brought camellias to the United States.

The Alabama state seal has a map.

The map on the seal shows the main rivers of Alabama.

This is the state flag of Alabama. It is red and white.

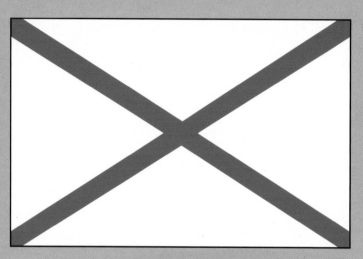

Schools in Alabama must fly the flag every school day.

13

The state bird of Alabama is the northern flicker. Northern flickers are woodpeckers. They are also called yellowhammers.

A flicker can make a hole in wood 16 inches deep.

This is a city in Alabama.
It is named Montgomery.
Montgomery is the
state capital.

People can ride around
Montgomery in electric
streetcars.

Marble is the Alabama state rock. Statues and buildings can be made from marble.

The Lincoln Memorial is made from Alabama marble.

Alabama has ocean, beaches,
rivers, and streams.

People visit Alabama
to have fun at the water.

ALABAMA FACTS

These pages provide detailed information that expands on the interesting facts found in the book. These pages are intended to be used by adults as a learning support to help young readers round out their knowledge of each state in the *Explore the U.S.A.* series.

Pages 4–5

Alabama has three unofficial nicknames. One is the Yellowhammer State. Yellowhammer was the nickname given to Confederate soldiers during the Civil War because of the brilliant yellow cloth on their new uniforms. It is also the common name of the state bird. Alabama may also be called the Cotton State and The Heart of Dixie.

Pages 6–7

On December 14, 1819, Alabama became the 22nd state to join the United States. Georgia, Tennessee, Mississippi, and Florida all border Alabama. Alabama is at the geographic center of the group of states that make up the South. There are 17 major rivers and more than 77,000 miles (124,000 kilometers) of river in Alabama.

Pages 8–9

Huntsville, Alabama, is known as "The Rocket City." The Saturn V rocket was designed, built, and tested at the Marshall Space Flight Center. Workers from all 67 Alabama counties helped develop the Saturn V. This rocket took the *Apollo 11* mission astronauts to the Moon in 1969. It traveled at nearly 25,000 miles (40,000 km) per hour.

Pages 10–11

The Alabama state flower was the goldenrod, until some people declared it a weed and wanted it changed. Camellias are not native to the United States. European explorers brought them from Asia. The Alabama state seal was designed in 1819 and used for 50 years. Then, a new seal was made with an eagle and banner stating, "Here We Rest." It was used for 71 years. In 1931, the original seal was returned to use.

Pages 12–13

The Alabama state flag was approved in 1895. The red bars cross over a white background to form St. Andrew's Cross. A law passed in 1923 stated that both the Alabama flag and the U.S. flag must be displayed in all public schools every day that school is in session. In 2001, the law was updated to include county courthouses, state offices, and municipal buildings.

Pages 14–15

The Yellowhammer is also called the southern flicker and the yellow-shafted flicker. Yellowhammers are unusual because they walk on the ground more than other woodpeckers. They travel using a series of hops. Confederate soldier veterans wore yellowhammer feathers on their hats or jackets when gathering to meet.

Pages 16–17

Montgomery had the first citywide trolley system in the United States. In April 1886, the first electric streetcar trolleys were rolled out in Montgomery. Called the Lightning Route, the system operated until 1936, when it was replaced by buses. Replicas of these trolleys are now used to take people on tours of the city's historic sites.

Pages 18–19

Four major monuments in Washington, D.C., are made from Alabama marble. These include the Washington Monument, the bust of Abraham Lincoln at the United States Capitol building, the Lincoln Memorial, and the U.S. Supreme Court building. More than 30 million tons (27 million tonnes) of marble have been dug from Alabama since 1900.

Pages 20–21

The Alabama Gulf Coast is dotted with beaches that have sand as white as sugar. Tourists enjoy activities such as building sand castles, swimming, and boat tours to see ocean life such as bottlenose dolphins. People also boat and fish on the many lakes and rivers in Alabama. There are more than 100 campgrounds in the state.

KEY WORDS

Research has shown that as much as 65 percent of all written material published in English is made up of 300 words. These 300 words cannot be taught using pictures or learned by sounding them out. They must be recognized by sight. This book contains 47 common sight words to help young readers improve their reading fluency and comprehension. This book also teaches young readers several important content words, such as proper nouns. These words are paired with pictures to aid in learning and improve understanding.

Page	Sight Words First Appearance
5	a, from, given, is, it, name, state, the, this, to, was
7	four, in, next, of, part, where
8	Earth, first, people, than, that, three, took, went
11	has, on, rivers, shows
12	and, day, every, must, schools, white
15	also, are, can, make, they
16	around, city
19	be, made
20	at, have, water

Page	Content Words First Appearance
5	Alabama, soldiers, Yellowhammer
7	Gulf of Mexico, shape, United States
8	minutes, Moon, rocket, space, workers
11	camellia, explorers, flower, map, seal
12	flag
15	bird, hole, northern flicker, wood, woodpeckers
16	capital, Montgomery, streetcars
19	buildings, Lincoln Memorial, marble, rock, statues
20	beaches, oceans, streams

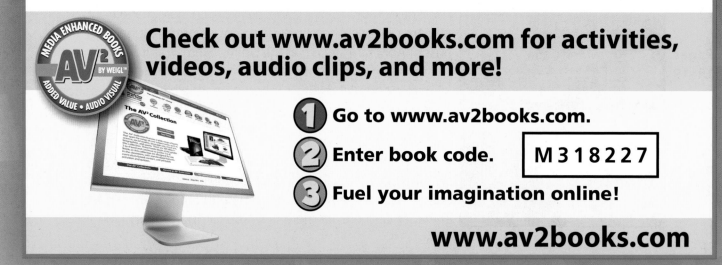

Check out www.av2books.com for activities, videos, audio clips, and more!

1 Go to www.av2books.com.

2 Enter book code. M 3 1 8 2 2 7

3 Fuel your imagination online!

www.av2books.com